Lydia Ramsey's Little Book of Table Manners

—⚔—

85 Tips on Dining for Success

LONGFELLOW PRESS
2008

How To Use This Book

- Follow the tips to advance your own career.

- Package this book as a value-added bonus with a product you sell.

- Distribute this book to your sales team.

- Customize this book and offer it as a "give away" at corporate or association seminars.

- Make it part of the curriculum in a business training session.

- Give it as a gift to new hires.

- Send it to university and business school students to market your company as a prospective employer.

- Give it as a gift to a recent college graduate.

Introduction

So much business is conducted over meals today that the successful professional dares not venture out without knowing good table manners.

Whether the purpose of the meal is to win over a customer, enhance a client relationship, impress a potential employer, or acquire a promotion, you want to feel confident and at ease in any dining situation. This includes everything from knowing which meal is appropriate for the business you need to conduct, to understanding your role as either host or guest and being competent with the foods and utensils that you encounter.

You can't concentrate on the business at a hand if you are worried about which fork to use, how to eat the pasta or what to do with that olive pit in your mouth. Use these 85 tips to ensure that your business dining is always a success.

Contents

The Role
of the
Host/Hostess

1. Choose a restaurant where you know the food and service are good and the atmosphere is conducive to conducting business.

2. Make arrangements ahead of time to take care of the bill.

3. Confirm the time and place either the day before the meal or that day.

4. Give your guest the prime seat—the one with the view.

5. Make suggestions about what to order.

6. Wait until your order has been taken before you begin discussing business.

The Role
of the
Guest

7. Ask your host for suggestions about what to order.

8. Stay in a moderate price range.

9. Remember that the person paying for the meal decides when to talk business.

10. Send a handwritten note the next day to thank your host.

Beginning The Business Meal

11. Remember that business meals are not about the food—they are about business first.

12. Wait until everyone has been served and your host has started to eat before you begin.

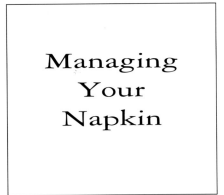

Managing
Your
Napkin

13. Leave your napkin on the table until everyone is seated.

14. Place the large dinner napkin in your lap with the fold toward your waist.

15. The smaller luncheon napkin is opened fully and placed in your lap.

16. Put your napkin back on the table after everyone has finished eating and is ready to leave the table.

17. If you need to excuse yourself during the meal, do so between courses, and put your napkin on your chair.

18. Use your napkin for blotting your mouth, nothing else.

Navigating The Place Setting

19. The place setting is your guide to the meal when the meal is pre-ordered.

20. Forks belong on the left, and knives and spoons on the right.

21. Use your utensils from the outside in, starting with the soupspoon on the far right or the salad fork on your far left.

22. Glasses are placed on the right above your knife. The bread and butter plate is on the left above the fork.

23. Soup is spooned away from you toward the back of the bowl.

24. The only crackers you may crumble in your soup are the oyster crackers.

25. When resting between mouthfuls, you may leave your soupspoon in the bowl.

26. When you have finished, place the spoon on the saucer or plate under the bowl.

Buttering
Your
Bread

27. Your bread and butter plate is on the left side of your place setting.

28. Break off only one or two bite-size pieces of bread at a time.

29. Place the butter on your plate with the main butter knife, and use your butter knife to spread the butter on your bread.

30. Butter one small piece of bread at a time, not half the roll at once.

Passing
Foods

31. Pass foods to the right because the wait staff is serving from the left.

32. If you are closest to an item that needs to be passed, such as the basket of rolls; pick up the basket, offer the bread to the person on your left, take a piece for yourself and pass it to the person on your right.

33. When you pass a serving dish with a handle, make sure the handle is facing the person to whom you are handing the dish.

34. Pass the salt and pepper together even if the other person only asks for one.

Holding
Your
Utensils

35. Hold your fork as you would a pencil.

36. Use the knife for cutting, not sawing.

37. The utensils are used for eating, not for gesturing.

38. Used knives, forks, and spoons are never placed on the table.

39. If you drop a utensil, let the waiter pick it up and bring you a clean one.

40. Cut your food and eat it one piece at a time.

Understanding Continental and American Styles of Eating

41. The AMERICAN STYLE of eating is the zigzag method. You hold the fork in your left hand and the knife in your right hand to cut your food.

When you have finished cutting, you put the knife down on your plate, and switch the fork to your right hand to take the food to your mouth.

42. When you eat CONTINENTAL STYLE, you cut your food in the same manner as American; however, you keep the fork in your left hand and take the food to your mouth with the tines down.

27

43. In Continental style, it is not necessary to place the knife on the plate while taking food to your mouth.

44. Be careful not to wave your knife or fork around or use them as props.

45. Eating Continental or American style is your choice. The only requirement is that you be consistent. If you begin eating Continental Style, you must finish that way. Switching mid-course is not acceptable.

Resting & Finished Positions

46. Where you place your utensils on your plate indicates whether you are resting between bites or have finished eating and are waiting for your plate to be removed.

47. To indicate that you are resting between

bites, place your knife horizontally at the top of your plate, blade facing in. Your fork is placed in the lower right hand portion of your plate.

Resting position, American style

48. When you have finished, bring the knife down to rest beside the fork in the lower right-hand corner.

Finished position, American style (tines up)

49. If you choose to eat Continental style, the knife is in the same position for resting as with the American style; but the fork rests in the lower left-hand corner of the plate with the tines down.

Resting position, Continental style (tines down)

50. The Continental style finished position is identical to American style except that the fork tines face down.

Finished position, Continental style (tines down)

Drinking Water and Wine, Coffee and Tea

51. The water is for sipping, not for washing down your food.

52. The water glass is the largest one on the table. There must be a reason.

53. The red wine goblet is larger than the white wine goblet.

54. Hold a white wine glass by the stem and a red wine glass by the bowl.

55. Alcoholic beverages should be avoided during business meals or taken in moderation.

56. When you add packaged sweetener to your beverage, tear the packet only about two-thirds of the way across.

57. Use no more than two packets of sweetener, and open them separately.

58. Avoid clinking your spoon on the cup or glass.

59. Rest the used spoon in the saucer.

60. Coffee is meant to be drunk after the meal, not during.

61. Do not turn your cup upside down in your saucer to indicate that you do not want coffee unless the server asks you to as a signal to the person pouring the coffee.

62. Chewing ice at the table or spitting it back in the glass is not acceptable adult business behavior.

Finishing
Off The
Meal

63. If the table is preset, your dessert fork and spoon will be placed at the top of your place setting.

64. Move the dessert fork and spoon into place when your dessert arrives.

65. Pace your eating. Pay attention to how fast or slow the other diners are eating so you do not finish way ahead of them or lag behind.

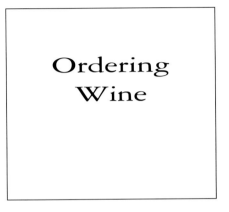

Ordering
Wine

66. If you are not totally confident about ordering wine, call upon the wine steward or a knowledgeable server. Just be sure that your wine expert is indeed an expert, and not the college kid who was hired yesterday.

67. To avoid confusion over pronunciation of foreign wines, use the bin number printed next to the name of the wine. There is less room for error when you order # 212 rather than the *Chateau Larose Trintaudon Medoc.*

68. When the wine is brought to the table, the server will hold the bottle up for you to verify that it is in fact the one that you ordered.

69. There is no need to sniff the cork. Just check to see if it is dry or moist. If a wine bottle has been stored properly, the cork will be moist.

70. Send the wine back only if there is something wrong with it, not because you aren't wild about your choice. Just order a different bottle next time.

71. The red wine glass is larger than the white wine glass and is held by the bowl rather than the stem. The white wine glass is held by the stem so as not to warm the wine.

72. As the host, it is your duty to see that your guests' wine glasses are refilled, either by you or the server.

73. The rule of drinking white wine with fish and red wine with red meat no longer applies except at very formal dinners.

Tipping

74. The word "tip" originated as an acronym for the phrase, "To Insure Promptness." Obviously, it began as a way of guaranteeing quality service. Today, however, tips are expected in most cases, regardless of level of service.

75. Today the expected tip is 15% to 20%. Tip 15% in a moderately priced restaurant.

76. In an upscale restaurant, the customary amount is 20% because there are several servers, including the captain and busboy, who will share in the tip.

77. The captain usually receives 5% and the waiter 15%. The busboy is not tipped by the customer, but by the captain or waiter.

78. Another thorny little question that arises is whether to include or exclude the sales tax

when figuring the tip. The choice is yours, but it is perfectly acceptable to figure the tip minus the sales tax.

79. The valet who parks your car also deserves a tip. Depending upon the restaurant, give him one or two dollars. The more upscale the establishment, the higher the tip.

80. The coatroom clerk should receive a tip of one dollar a coat and 50 cents for each additional coat.

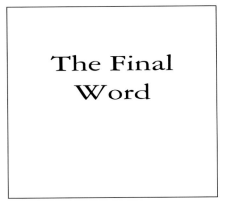

The Final
Word

81. If food lands on the table, pick it up as discreetly as possible, and put it back on your plate.

82. If you have special dietary issues, let this be known ahead of time for pre-ordered meals.

83. Women should excuse themselves from the table to reapply makeup.

84. Never ask for a doggy bag at the business meal.

85. Handbags, keys and other personal items do not belong on the table.

TABLE MANNERS

About the Author

Lydia Ramsey is a business etiquette expert and a professional speaker and author. She is the president and founder of Manners That Sell, a Savannah-based firm offering keynotes and seminars on business etiquette and protocol to corporations, non-profit organizations, colleges and universities. She is the author of several books including *Manners That Sell: Adding the Polish That Builds Profits*; a syndicated columnist; and a contributor to business journals and trade publications across the country.

Lydia Ramsey has been featured and quoted in newspapers and magazines including *The New York Times, The Wall Street Journal, Entrepreneur, Inc., The Los Angeles Times, Real Simple Magazine, Cosmopolitan, Woman's Day, Men's Health, Men's Fitness* and *Golf Digest*. She is a frequent guest on national radio and television shows that include NPR's Motley Fool, "Stranded with Cash Peters" on the Travel Channel, PBS Television and the Paul Harvey Show. Ramsey recently worked with Voice of America Broadcasting, writing scripts to teach etiquette and English to young Chinese professionals.

Invite Lydia Ramsey to speak at your next event!

Phone her at 912-598-9812, e-mail her at
lydia@mannersthatsell.com or visit her website at
mannersthatsell.com

ISBN 0978-0-9670012-1-0 New
Lydia Ramsey's Little Book of Table Manners

Printed in Canada

Lydia Ramsey Inc.
1 Longfellow Lane
Savannah, Georgia 31411
Tel: 912.598.9812
e-mail: lydia@mannersthatsell.com
website: mannersthatsell.com